STICKMEN'S GUIDE
TO
TECHNOLOGY

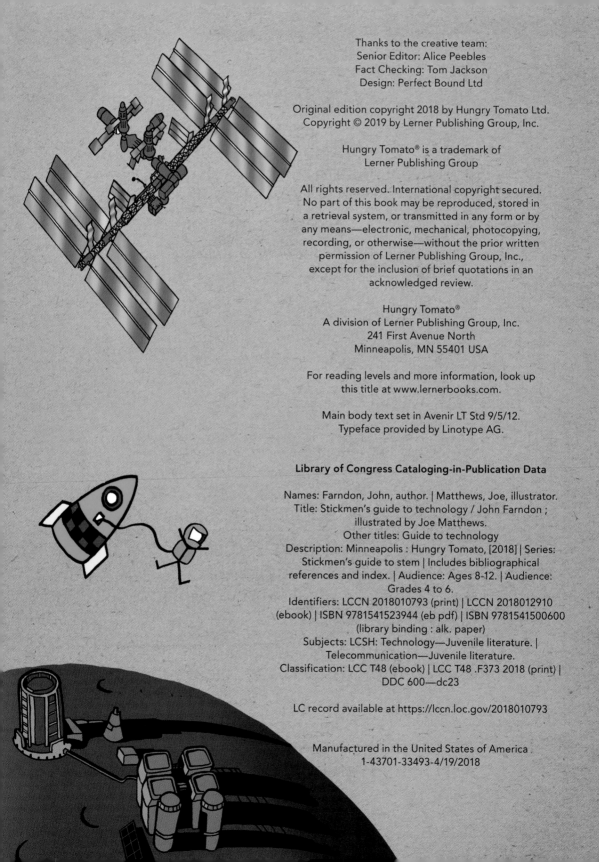

Thanks to the creative team:
Senior Editor: Alice Peebles
Fact Checking: Tom Jackson
Design: Perfect Bound Ltd

Hungry Tomato®
A division of Lerner Publishing Group, Inc.
241 First Avenue North
Minneapolis, MN 55401 USA

For reading levels and more information, look up
this title at www.lernerbooks.com.

Main body text set in Avenir LT Std 9/5/12.
Typeface provided by Linotype AG.

Library of Congress Cataloging-in-Publication Data

Names: Farndon, John, author. | Matthews, Joe, illustrator.
Title: Stickmen's guide to technology / John Farndon ;
illustrated by Joe Matthews.
Other titles: Guide to technology
Description: Minneapolis : Hungry Tomato, [2018] | Series:
Stickmen's guide to stem | Includes bibliographical
references and index. | Audience: Ages 8-12. | Audience:
Grades 4 to 6.
Identifiers: LCCN 2018010793 (print) | LCCN 2018012910
(ebook) | ISBN 9781541523944 (eb pdf) | ISBN 9781541500600
(library binding : alk. paper)
Subjects: LCSH: Technology—Juvenile literature. |
Telecommunication—Juvenile literature.
Classification: LCC T48 (ebook) | LCC T48 .F373 2018 (print) |
DDC 600—dc23

LC record available at https://lccn.loc.gov/2018010793

Manufactured in the United States of America
1-43701-33493-4/19/2018

STICKMEN'S GUIDE

TO

TECHNOLOGY

by John Farndon

Illustrated by Joe Matthews

HUNGRY TOMATO®

Minneapolis

Meet your new puppy, Chip the robot dog. You can even train him to do tricks!

Contents

About Technology   6

Life Changing   8

Know All   10

Tiny, Tiny   12

Self Control   14

Look Over   16

Atomic   18

Look Out   20

Doctor Tech   22

Out of This World   24

Other Worlds   26

Timeline of Technology   28

Techie!   30

Glossary   31

Index   32

About Technology

Technology is all the clever ways people come up with for making things work. It's about ingenious machines and processes. It's about using scientific knowledge and practical knowhow to think up new inventions and methods of dealing with practical problems. It's what makes the modern world tick . . .

What does technology do?

Technology is about finding practical solutions to problems and finding ways to perform practical tasks better. For instance, you might want to get lots of people to the top of a mountain quickly every day. So technologists devise a cable car.

Changing technology

Technology is always changing. Once, gas-engined cars seemed like a brilliant technology for enabling people to move quickly anywhere they want. But now we know that the pollution they cause damages the world's climate. So technologists are developing new and cleaner ways of powering cars, such as electric motors and hydrogen fuel cells.

Cutting-edge technology

The very latest developments in technology are calling cutting-edge technology. That's because they seem like the very edge of the blade of a knife, cutting through today's problems to find exciting new solutions. Electric flying taxis are cutting-edge technology that may soon become a reality.

High tech

High tech is the most complicated and clever technology that only specialists can create. Typically, it means technology that needs very sophisticated electronic systems, such as robotics, the latest computers, nuclear weapons systems, hospital scanners, and so on. California's Silicon Valley is one of the hubs of high-tech development.

New technology

Every now and then, ideas emerge that open up entirely new areas of technology. It's not always easy to predict which will develop. But here are a few that might: driverless trucks, computers that can teach themselves, **gene** therapy (illnesses cured by altering genes), and face recognition (electronic systems that can identify you from your face alone).

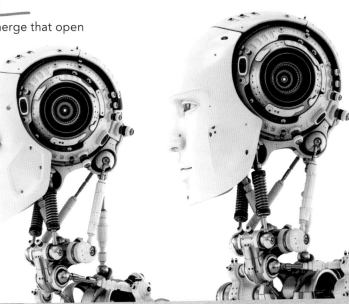

Life Changing

Did you know that with genetic modification (GM), farmers may one day grow chocolate-flavored strawberries? Or that goat's milk may be used for bulletproof vests? Genes are the chemical instructions that tell living things how to live and grow. GM is how scientists alter them to make things grow in different ways.

Going for growth

Genes are strips of **DNA**, the chemical molecule inside every living cell that carries life's instructions. Each gene gives a living thing a particular characteristic. To make a change, scientists find a gene that gives the right quality in another organism. They then snip this out chemically and insert it into the DNA of the organism they want to modify.

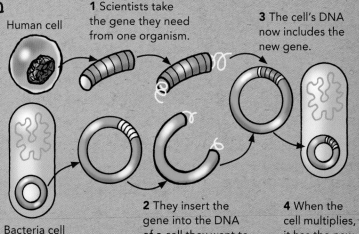

1 Scientists take the gene they need from one organism.

3 The cell's DNA now includes the new gene.

Human cell

2 They insert the gene into the DNA of a cell they want to modify.

4 When the cell multiplies, it has the new characteristic.

Bacteria cell

What changes

Bacteria and yeast are typically modified to make them into tiny factories, creating lots of a particular natural chemical as they multiply, such as human growth hormone or insulin. Farm crops and occasionally animals are modified to give them qualities that will help them grow better.

Yeast

Bacteria

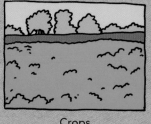

Crops

Animals

New plants

Cotton, potatoes, and other crops have been given a "Bt" gene to make them poisonous to insects that usually eat them. Some people believe that GM will give us more food to help us feed the world's hungry. But others argue that changing genes could have terrible, unforeseen effects on wildlife.

Copy sheep

An animal born naturally has a mix of genes from its mother and father, and so a mix of their characteristics. But animals can be cloned. Cloning means they grow from DNA taken from just one animal, so they are identical copies. The first cloned farm animal was a sheep called Dolly born in 1996.

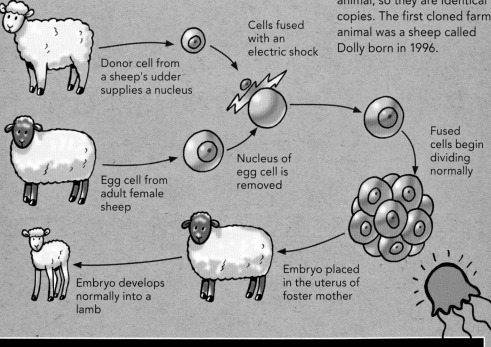

Donor cell from a sheep's udder supplies a nucleus

Cells fused with an electric shock

Egg cell from adult female sheep

Nucleus of egg cell is removed

Fused cells begin dividing normally

Embryo develops normally into a lamb

Embryo placed in the uterus of foster mother

Glowing mice

GM can give animals and plants qualities they never had before. Some mice and other animals have been given a gene that makes jellyfish glow in the dark. So the mice glow in the dark too! Maybe in future, there will be people who glow in the dark . . .

Know All

Computers are already used for an incredibly wide range of tasks, from running train networks to creating films and music—not to mention the internet. And they've only just got started . . .

Your bathroom mirror will give medical advice after scanning your body.

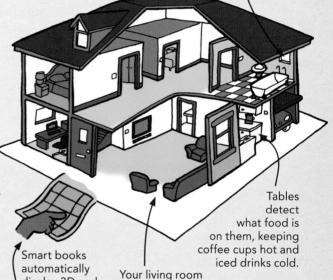

Smart fabrics will adjust the warmth of your clothes to suit the temperature.

Linked-in house

Until recently, the internet was only a way of communicating between computers and smartphones. But experts expect the **internet of things** to expand dramatically. This connects the internet to ordinary items around the home and office, from fridges to TVs, so that your fridge, for example, could detect when you run out of milk and order it online.

Smart books automatically display 3D and virtual reality pictures.

Your living room might surround you with sights and sounds from your friend's house or the Amazon jungle.

Tables detect what food is on them, keeping coffee cups hot and iced drinks cold.

Number crunchers

A computer handles data in four stages: input, memory, processing, and output. In the memory and processor, everything is converted to calculations and works by switching patterns of electronic circuits. A computer can only switch electric circuits on or switch them off. So all its operating instructions are in simple binary (or two-part) code, normally written as 0s and 1s.

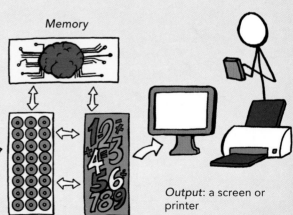

Memory

Input: a keyboard or camera

Processor: control unit and arithmetic logic unit

Output: a screen or printer

1 You type the address of the computer or website you wish to link to—or do an address search.

2 You tap "go" to send the request to your router.

3 The router sends the request to a central computer called an Internet Service Provider (ISP).

Connected world

The internet allows your computer to link to other computers all over the world. It all works via the World Wide Web. The web transforms computer output into simple web pages that can be read and displayed by any computer accessing the internet. More than three billion people are connected to the internet, so that's a lot of computing power!

6 The website sends a signal via the hub, your ISP and your router to display the website on your computer—in less than a second.

5 The hub sends data packets to the website, asking to connect to the website.

4 The ISP sends the request to a hub, a high-powered computer junction that searches for the right link.

What will the weather be?

Some of the world's most powerful computers are involved in predicting how climate may change in the future. Scientists feed in huge amounts of data about how weather has changed in the past, then get the computer to run these changes into the future. In this way, NASA scientists predict how global temperatures will change.

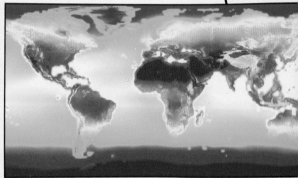

Superbrain

The world's fastest computer—and the first one as fast as a human brain—is the gigantic Sunway TaihuLight in China. It can perform 93 million billion operations a second. Scientists are using it to recreate the very first moments of the universe.

Taihu is as fast as a human brain, but soon supercomputers may be as fast as a city full of brains!

Tiny, Tiny

With a powerful microscope, you can see some amazingly small things, from bacteria to the hair cells on a fly. But there's a whole new scale of much smaller things called the nanoscale. Scientists are exploring this to see if they can create the tiniest machines and material structures ever. This is called nanotechnology.

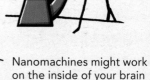

Onsite repairs

Just imagine—in the future, there may be tiny nanomachines that can be sent inside your body to see what's wrong, and even make repairs on the spot. Little robot submarines could travel around in your blood and send signals back to tell doctors just what's going on. Here's some of the things nanotechnology might do (right).

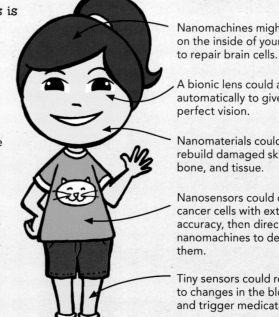

Nanomachines might work on the inside of your brain to repair brain cells.

A bionic lens could adjust automatically to give you perfect vision.

Nanomaterials could rebuild damaged skin, bone, and tissue.

Nanosensors could detect cancer cells with extreme accuracy, then direct nanomachines to destroy them.

Tiny sensors could respond to changes in the blood and trigger medication.

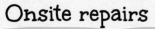

Water molecule	10^{-1} nm
Gold atom	3×10^{-1} nm
Glucose molecule	1 nm
Haemoglobin	5 nm
Virus	100 nm
Bacteria	1,000 nm
Blood cells	1,000 nm
Hair	100,000 nm
Ant	10^6 nm
Baseball	10^8 nm

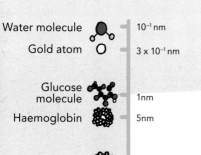

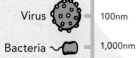

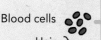

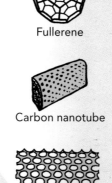

Fullerene

Carbon nanotube

Graphene

How small is nano?

You might think a strand of your hair is pretty thin. Or that bacteria are seriously tiny. But on the nanoscale, hairs are like fat tree trunks and bacteria are like footballs. A nanometer (nm) is a billionth of a meter. A hair is actually 100,000 nm across. Scientists are now making nanomaterials of carbon, such as fullerene balls, graphene sheets, and superstrong nanotube fibers.

Images not to scale

It's a stick-up

Geckos can hang on to almost any surface. This is because of tiny forces created between the surface and countless nanoscale projections on hairs on the geckos' feet. Scientists have used this idea to create "gecko tape," which clings to any surface. They hung a toy Spider-Man to glass with this. Now scientists have gecko gloves that let them climb up sheer glass walls.

Seeing tiny

Special, superpowerful electron microscopes let you see things such as the multiple eyes of a fly. But to see and change things on the nanoscale, scientists have developed even more powerful magnifiers called Atomic Force Microscopes (AFMs) and Scanning Tunneling Microscopes (STMs), which use special electronic effects. With these, they can push atoms around and arrange them to make tiny machines.

Cutting-edge technology

When knights came up against Muslim warriors in the medieval crusades, they found the Muslims had swords made of Damascus steel. These swords were so sharp, they could slice through a silk scarf floating through the air (as well as a knight). Recently, scientists found that they owed their sharpness to carbon nanotubes in the steel created by the special forging process.

Self Control

Mechanical moving figures, called automatons, date back thousands of years. But with computer technology we can now build clever robots. Robots are machines run by electronic programs that can do complex tasks by themselves. There are already robots making cars and exploring volcanoes. In the future, maybe robots will look and even think like us!

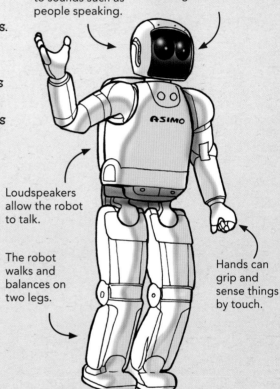

Microphones in the ears respond to sounds such as people speaking.

Cameras in the eyes respond to visual input, recognizing faces and reading books.

Loudspeakers allow the robot to talk.

The robot walks and balances on two legs.

Hands can grip and sense things by touch.

Bots are us

All robots have three main elements: a controller or "brain," mechanical parts such as motors and grippers, and sensors that respond to changes. They can be built in any shape. But many robot makers want to make a "humanoid" robot the same shape as us, with two legs and two arms, like the famous Japanese Asimo and French Nao robots.

Bots to the rescue

Robots are now being built to perform rescue missions because they can go where it is too dangerous for people to go. They might find buried earthquake victims or carry medical supplies to people who are trapped. Robots shaped like snakes, called snakebots, can slither under piles of rubble or through pipes on rescue missions.

Robotoys

More and more robots are being made as toys. For those who cannot have a real dog, Chip the robot dog could be a good alternative. Chip follows you around in a puppylike way, with advanced sensors for finding its way around obstacles. It responds to commands. You can even train it to do tricks.

Space bots

At the moment, it is impossible for humans to go to Mars and come back. But robots like Curiosity Rover can be landed there. Curiosity can move around the planet's surface on its six wheels, beaming back pictures and picking up samples for analysis. In 2018, Curiosity found some rock samples with squiggles which some say are possibly fossils of microscopic life.

Roboanimals

Animals have evolved over millions of years to be very good at certain things, so robot makers are beginning to look to them for ideas. Here are some of the other robot animals that scientists are developing. They may not look much like the animals, but they move and behave in the same way.

Robot ants can move together in a swarm to pull things as big as cars.

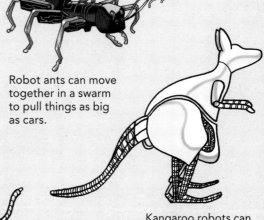

Kangaroo robots can jump like real kangaroos, but tirelessly.

Robot cheetahs are the fastest running robots, reaching nearly 30 mph (50 km/h). They can jump over fences.

Robot butterflies flutter through the air just like real butterflies.

Full-sized robot horses can use special sensors to track criminals across snow, ice, and rocky terrain.

Look Over

We live in a world full of electronic pictures. Cameras on our phones allow us to record everyday moments at the touch of a button. But there are many other kinds of electronic pictures, from airport security scans to thermal images, which allow police to chase suspects in pitch darkness by detecting body heat.

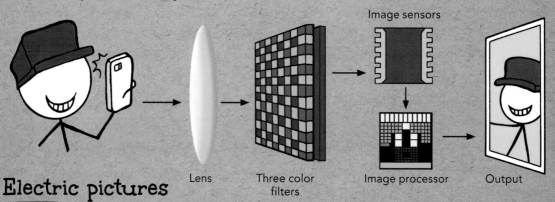

Lens | Three color filters | Image sensors | Image processor | Output

Electric pictures

Inside your phone there is a rectangle made up of lots of tiny **photo cells**. When you take a picture, the phone's lens projects a picture on to the cells. The cells respond instantly by sending tiny electric signals that match the pattern of light in the picture. These signals are stored in the phone's memory or display the picture by using the electricity to make a glowing pattern on the screen.

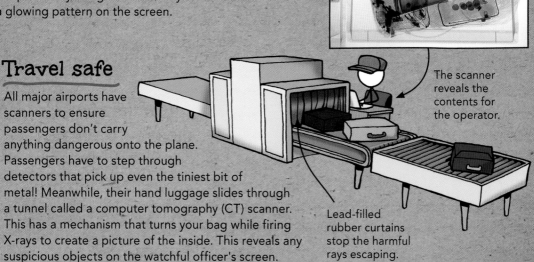

The scanner reveals the contents for the operator.

Travel safe

All major airports have scanners to ensure passengers don't carry anything dangerous onto the plane. Passengers have to step through detectors that pick up even the tiniest bit of metal! Meanwhile, their hand luggage slides through a tunnel called a computer tomography (CT) scanner. This has a mechanism that turns your bag while firing X-rays to create a picture of the inside. This reveals any suspicious objects on the watchful officer's screen.

Lead-filled rubber curtains stop the harmful rays escaping.

Storm warning!

Doppler radar detects things by bouncing microwaves off them. It then builds up a picture from the pattern of waves bouncing back. With a special kind of doppler radar, storm watchers can build up a detailed map of where and how much rain is falling. Doppler radar can even give an indication of wind speed.

Microwaves bounce off drops of water and ice. They are detected by the scanner below.

Doppler radar sends out microwaves.

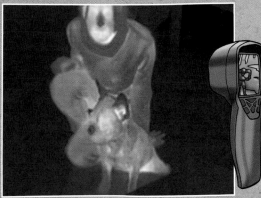

Seeing hot

When things are hot, they send out invisible infrared rays. These are like a glowing light, but you cannot see them. They can be detected on **thermal imaging** cameras, though. Cameras like these can show people in pitch darkness because of their body heat. Police often use them to catch criminals who think they are hidden by darkness.

Thermal imager

Can't see me!

Scientists are also developing devices to make things invisible. You may think an invisibility cloak is just Harry Potter magic. But scientists are now developing "meta" materials that divert light rays—and really could make you invisible!

Atomic

Atoms are seriously tiny. But the energy that binds together the nucleus or core of an atom is stupendous. By releasing the energy from the nuclei of millions of atoms, nuclear power stations can generate a lot of power.

Power from atoms

Inside a nuclear reactor are rods of uranium fuel. When the power station starts to operate, engineers start a **chain reaction** in the rods (below). Special **control rods** soak up some of the stray particles. They get hot and heat water to make steam that drives turbines that generate electricity.

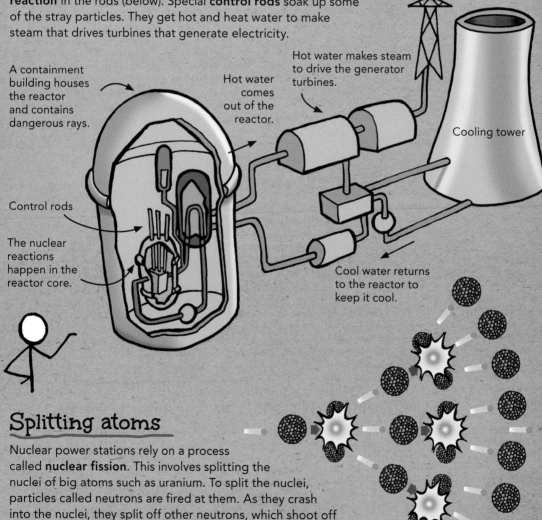

A containment building houses the reactor and contains dangerous rays.

Control rods

The nuclear reactions happen in the reactor core.

Hot water comes out of the reactor.

Hot water makes steam to drive the generator turbines.

Cooling tower

Cool water returns to the reactor to keep it cool.

Splitting atoms

Nuclear power stations rely on a process called **nuclear fission**. This involves splitting the nuclei of big atoms such as uranium. To split the nuclei, particles called neutrons are fired at them. As they crash into the nuclei, they split off other neutrons, which shoot off to split other nuclei. And so it all spreads in a chain reaction.

Nuclear waste

The big problem with nuclear power is that the fuel, once used, becomes highly radioactive; that is, it sends out dangerous rays. When it first comes out of the reactor, it would kill anyone close in seconds. It remains radioactive for thousands of years. No one yet knows what to do with the waste. Mostly it is hidden in special cases underground (right). But these may leak in time.

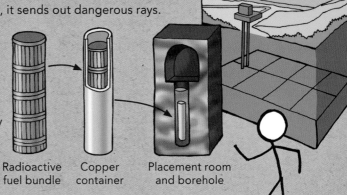

Radioactive fuel bundle

Copper container

Placement room and borehole

Nuclear fusion process

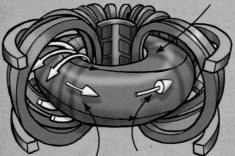

Torus

Magnets send the gas particles around and around.

Speeding gas particles smash together to release power.

Forced together

Scientists are working to get nuclear power from **nuclear fusion**—that is, by forcing together small atoms like deuterium (a kind of gas). This is the process that makes stars burn bright. Scientists are trying to do it inside a ring-shaped tunnel called a torus. If they succeed, they can make a lot of power without dangerous waste.

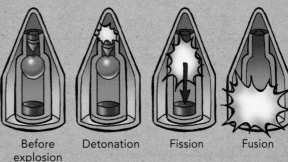

Before explosion

Detonation

Fission

Fusion

Explosive power

The most devastating bombs ever made combine nuclear fission and nuclear fusion. They are called hydrogen bombs and start with an explosive fission chain reaction. This forces hydrogen atoms together in the core of the bomb to unleash an even more terrible fusion explosion. Fortunately, they have only ever been exploded for tests.

Look Out

Every now and then, places around the world are hit by extreme natural disasters such as hurricanes, volcano eruptions, earthquakes, tsunamis, and floods. There is a much better chance of people escaping if they can be warned in time. So scientists and technologists are working to set up warning systems.

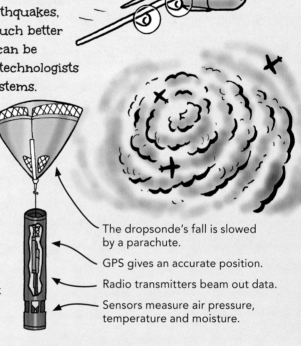

Hurricane watch

Every year, hurricanes sweep across the Atlantic and Pacific. Scientists can follow their path from satellites high above them. But they cannot measure conditions deep inside the storm. So planes are flown right into the storm to make observations and drop tubes called dropsondes that send data back to storm watchers.

The dropsonde's fall is slowed by a parachute.

GPS gives an accurate position.

Radio transmitters beam out data.

Sensors measure air pressure, temperature and moisture.

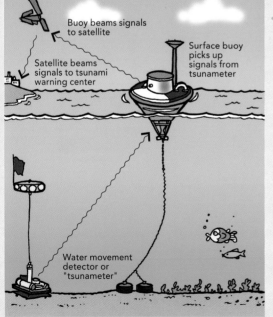

Buoy beams signals to satellite

Satellite beams signals to tsunami warning center

Surface buoy picks up signals from tsunameter

Water movement detector or "tsunameter"

Tsunami warning

Tsunamis are huge waves set off by undersea earthquakes. They move very fast, and it is hard to know they are coming. So scientists try to give advance warning by setting up an array of buoys tethered above monitors placed on the sea floor. These detect any dramatic movement of the water and beam out a warning.

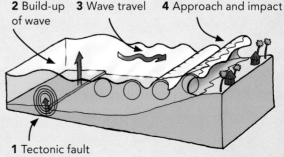

2 Build-up of wave   **3** Wave travel   **4** Approach and impact

1 Tectonic fault

Building safe

The biggest danger in an earthquake is from falling buildings. So in earthquake zones, tall buildings are often built in a way that will withstand quakes. They may not survive the most severe ones, but they can endure most minor quakes.

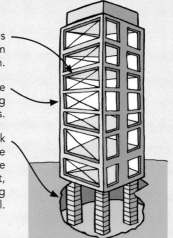

Cross-bracing gives walls maximum strength.

Steel bars in the walls reduce rocking movements.

Springlike shock absorbers under the building soak up the ground movement, so the building keeps still.

Changes in gases coming out of the volcano may indicate that magma is moving up the vent.

Drones, satellites, and helicopters look for changes from a safe distance.

Shaking of the ground detected by seismometers may show an eruption is imminent.

Meters may detect a slight change in the ground shape, indicating magma pushing up from below.

Volcano warnings

Volcanic eruptions are among the most terrifying of all natural disasters. But many cities are built close to volcanoes. So volcano experts look for warning signs that a volcano might erupt, such as pressure building up in the magma chamber beneath the volcano or unusual gases being released.

Flood warning

Floods can be slow to start but turn into the most devastating disasters of all because their effects are so widespread. The flood of the Yangtze River in China in 1931 was the worst ever natural disaster, killing 4 million people. Weather watchers join with river experts to try and warn people of a flood, but even with warning, they are not easy to escape.

Doctor Tech

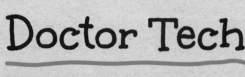

Technology plays a key part in looking after us. Clever machines and materials repair or replace damaged body parts. Scanners see inside the body and tell doctors if anything's wrong. Machines allow doctors to operate on a patient from far away. Robot doctors can even listen to patients to help find the problem!

Transmitter

Receiver implant inside eye

Camera

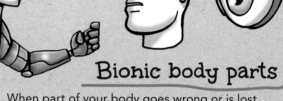

Passive bionics with a single purpose, such as a heart and hip joint

Active bionics with multiple purposes

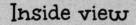

Bionic body parts

When part of your body goes wrong or is lost, maybe you can replace it with a mechanical bionic part. Some people already have artificial hearts, livers, legs, arms, and ears. One day, these parts may work better than the real thing, giving people superpowers. Blind people may one day be given sight by implanted video cameras (above).

A magnetic field pulls hydrogen particles in the body into alignment.

The scanner picks up the pattern of tiny radio signals that the particles send out as they swivel back to normal when the field is switched off.

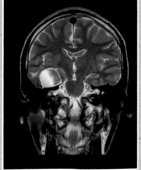

Inside view

Doctors can look inside your body to see if anything's wrong with clever scanners. CT (computerized tomography) scanners circle the patient, firing X-ray beams to make computer-generated images. These can reveal cancers and internal injuries. MRI (Magnetic Resonance Imaging) scanners can see things happening in your living brain!

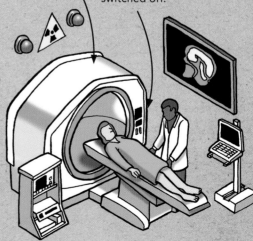

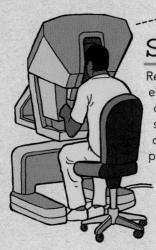

Surgery at a distance

Remote surgery technology may one day enable surgeons to carry out complex operations on patients from the other side of the world. Robot machinery on the spot actually works on the patient. But the surgeon guides it from far away, using **virtual reality** technology.

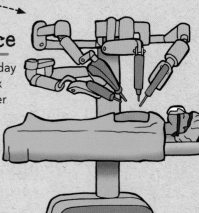

New for old

In the past, replacement body parts were made from materials like metal or plastic. Now biotechnologists are learning to grow new body parts from living cells so that they are just like the real thing. These are the stages in growing a whole new nose.

1 A scan builds a 3D picture of the nose wanted.

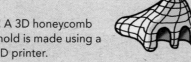

2 A 3D honeycomb mold is made using a 3D printer.

3 Special stem cells from the body are sprayed onto the mold.

4 The mold is dipped in nutrients so the cells grow into a cartilage nose.

5 The cartilage nose is attached to the body so that skin grows over it.

6 The new, skin-covered nose is fixed in place by surgeons.

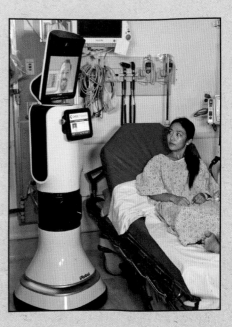

Doctor, doctor

Doctors are very busy. So some people think that in future when you go to see a doctor, you will see a robot instead. The robot will ask questions and take measurements, then diagnose the problem and decide the treatment or send you on to a human doctor.

Out of This World

Some of the most amazing technology is literally out of this world—it's the technology that has enabled us to explore space. Things that were once just science fiction are now reality, such as living in space stations far above Earth. One day, we may be able to send robots to mine asteroids or take day trips into space.

International Space Station

Space room

The International Space Station was carried into space bit by bit and put together over dozens of space flights. It now circles the globe every 90 minutes at a speed of about 17,500 mph (28,000 km/h). It is as big as a football field and zooms around Earth at 248 miles (400 km) above the ground. Since 2009, it has typically had a crew of six who stay up there for four to six months at a time.

Looking into the distance

Earth's atmosphere looks clear to us, but if you want to see faint, distant stars, it's like frosted glass. So astronomers send up special telescopes on satellites to look out from high above the atmosphere in space. The most famous of these space telescopes is the Hubble, launched in 1990. It is still sending back amazing pictures of galaxies on the other side of the universe.

Hubble space telescope

Hubble image of the Horsehead Nebula

Space holidays

Spaceflights are usually government projects, and outsiders are allowed aboard by special invitation. But space technologists are working on spaceplanes that might take ordinary paying customers into space. Virgin Galactic's *SpaceShip Two* will carry six passengers and could be in operation by 2020. But tickets cost $250,000!

Out and about

Space may be empty, but it's a dangerous place for humans, full of harmful rays and entirely lacking air. So if astronauts need to get outside their spacecraft to make repairs, they wear very elaborate protective suits called Extravehicular Mobility Units (EMUs).

Gold in the visor filters out dangerous rays from the Sun.

A heavy backpack contains air for breathing and water for cooling, as well as jetpacks.

Multiple layers protect the body from pressure problems, while tubes of circulating water help to stop the body boiling.

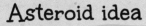

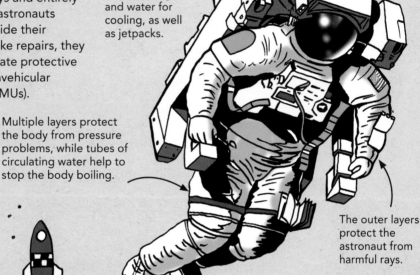

The outer layers protect the astronaut from harmful rays.

Asteroid idea

Asteroids are very rich in rare minerals such as gold, iridium, palladium, platinum, and tungsten. Engineers are working on ways to build robot spacecraft that could be sent to asteroids, extract the minerals, then send them back to Earth on carrier spacecraft. But this is such an expensive process that it is unlikely to prove worthwhile yet.

Other Worlds

Imagine riding a tiger or seeing a whale leap through your bedroom floor. Well, quite soon you may be able to have such experiences as if they are real. Computer technology can create these experiences, then immerse us in them so convincingly that they seem real.

Virtual reality

Virtual reality tricks your mind into thinking things are real by feeding signals into your senses. The main way is through stereoscopic display, which gives two slightly different views to each of your eyes. The views shift exactly as if things are real and solid—and change exactly as if you are moving through the scene for real. Some devices also move and shake your body to build up the whole illusion.

Lenses

Display

Circuit board

Solid light

Holograms are 3D photos made with laser beams. The beams are split in two with mirrors and lenses. One bounces off the subject being photographed and onto a photo receiver. The other, called the reference beam, shines directly on the receiver. The "interference" between the light waves in the two beams creates tiny stripes on the photo receiver. These create a shimmering effect in the photo that looks 3D.

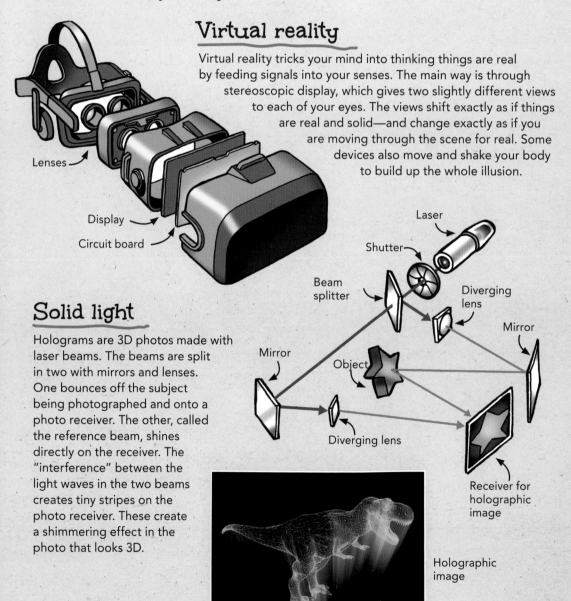

Laser

Shutter

Beam splitter

Diverging lens

Mirror

Mirror

Object

Diverging lens

Receiver for holographic image

Holographic image

Cyberspace

Cyberspace can simply mean the imaginary place where computer data is shared on the internet. But it can also mean the creation of new imaginary worlds by interacting computers in a form of virtual reality. Gamers already venture into these worlds when they play together online. You are really just manipulating the gaming controls, but it can seem as if you're fighting your opponent with real swords in a strange world.

Fantasy you

Online, you can already create an imaginary version of yourself called an avatar. You can do this by giving the characteristics you choose to a computer program that behaves like a person. In the future, your avatar might be so realistic and have so much detail about you that it seems real. Who knows, one day you might send your avatar to school, while you play at home!

Is that real?

One of the most exciting new technologies is augmented reality. Unlike virtual reality, this projects amazing computer-generated illusions so that they look as if they are happening in the real world. That's how you might get a whale leaping out of your classroom floor or keep your own pet dragon under the bed.

Timeline of Technology

One of the things that makes us human beings unique in the natural world is the way we use technology to solve problems. Other creatures occasionally use tools or build things, like beavers. But human technology is changing and developing rapidly all the time.

3.3 million years ago

Long ago, ape-like human ancestors, called australopithecines, learned to sharpen the edges of stones to make axes for cutting things such as meat and wood for building and weapons. Sharp.

1698CE

In England, Thomas Savery developed the first steam engine. Engines gave people the power to do things they'd never done before, like build giant factories and make trains and cars. Hissss.

1700   1800

9000BCE

The Stone Age (age of stone tools) ended with the discovery that metals could be melted out of rocks and used to make tools in any shape. It led first to the Bronze Age and then the Iron Age. Clang.

1804

British engineer Richard Trevithick built the first steam locomotive, the Pen-y-Darren. Just 26 years later, the first passenger trains ran between Liverpool and Manchester in England. Clackety clack.

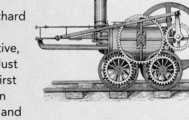

1826

In France, Nicéphore Niépce took the first photograph ever, recording the picture projected by a lens in chemicals coated on a metal plate that react to light. Snap.

1876

In Boston, Scottish inventor Alexander Graham Bell made the first ever telephone call, calling to his assistant in the next room: "Mr. Watson, come here. I want to see you." Ring ring.

1903

The Wright brothers took off in the Flyer in Kitty Hawk, North Carolina, for the first powered, controlled flight in an airplane. Weeee!

1900　　　　　　　**2000**

1888

German engineer Karl Benz built the first proper motor car for sale to the public. The Benz Patent-Motorwagen was a three-wheeler with a gas engine. Chugger chugger.

1961

On April 12, Soviet astronaut Yuri Gagarin became the first person to fly around the world in space, in the spacecraft Vostok 1. See the world (in 108 minutes)!

1989

British computer scientist Tim Berners-Lee invented the World Wide Web to enable computers to exchange data freely, and so launched the internet.

Techie!

Dick's steamer

The first steam locomotive was built by British engineer Richard Trevithick, known as Captain Dick. To prove it worked, Dick bet it could haul ten tons of coal nine miles along the Pen-y-Darren ironworks' railtracks, laid for horses to haul trains of wagons. In February 1804, the locomotive made its journey with ten tons, five wagons, and 70 men aboard. Dick won his bet, but the railway tracks cracked under the weight . . .

Flying butlers!

Englishman George Cayley invented aircraft wings, trying out his ideas with model gliders. In 1849, he launched a 10-year-old boy into the air for a short flight in one of his models, with "flappers" to propel himself along. Then in 1853, Cayley built a full-sized glider in which his terrified butler flew across a local valley, Brompton Dale. The butler survived and so made the world's first airplane flight.

Horsepower

When steam locomotives were invented, engineers had to prove they worked in public show trials. When Peter Cooper built the first American locomotive, *Tom Thumb*, in Baltimore in 1830, investors insisted he race it against a horse-drawn train. *Tom Thumb* was steaming ahead but then broke down, so the horse won the race. Fortunately for Cooper, investors had seen enough!

Tiny movie

Nanotechnology is the technology of very small things—things as small as atoms that can only be seen under very, very powerful microscopes. In 2013, nanotechnologists had fun by making the world's smallest movie, *A Boy and His Atom*. This short animated movie is made entirely by maneuvering carbon monoxide **molecules** with a scanning tunneling microscope, which magnifies them 100 million times!

Glossary

asteroid: a rock that orbits the sun—smaller and lumpier than a planet

bionic: describes artificial electronic or mechanical body parts

chain reaction: a series of events in a nuclear reaction. It starts when the splitting of one atom goes on to trigger the splitting of many more.

control rod: a rod that absorbs neutrons in a nuclear power plant to slow down chain reactions

DNA: the very long, twisted chemical molecule inside every living cell that carries life instructions in coded form

gene: short strips of DNA that carry the instructions for living organisms to make a particular feature

genetic modification or **GM:** the technology of giving living things different features by altering their genes

internet of things: the linking of electronic equipment so it can be controlled via the internet

molecule: the smallest particle of a chemical compound or element that exists separately

nanotechnology: technology of things so tiny that they can only be seen under the most powerful microscopes

nuclear fission: the release of nuclear energy by splitting large atoms

nuclear fusion: the release of nuclear energy by forcing together small atoms

photo cell: a tiny sensor that detects light, sending out a small electric current whenever light falls on it

thermal imaging: making pictures with devices that detect heat so you can see hot things, such as human bodies, in complete darkness

tsunami: a huge wave set off by an undersea earthquake

virtual reality: a 3D image made by a computer that people can interact with

Index

aircraft wings, 30
airplane flight, 29–30
airport security scanners, 16
asteroids, 25
Atomic Force Microscopes
 (AFMs), 13
augmented reality, 27
avatars, 27

body parts and repairs, 12,
 22–23

climate change predictions, 11
cloning, 9
computers, 10
CT scanners, 22
Curiosity Rover, 15
cutting-edge technology, 7
cyberspace, 27

Doppler radar, 17
dropsondes, 20

earthquake-resistant buildings,
 21

electric pictures, 16
Extravehicular Mobility Units
 (EMUs), 25

flood warning, 21

gecko gloves, 13
genetic modification (GM), 8–9

high tech, 7
holograms, 26
Hubble space telescope, 24
hurricane watching, 20
hydrogen bomb, 19

International Space Station, 24
internet, 11
internet of things, 10
invisibility devices, 17

MRI scanners, 22

nanotechnology, 12–13, 31
nuclear power, 18–19
nuclear waste, 19

remote surgery, 23
robots, 14–15, 23

Scanning Tunneling
 Microscopes (STMs), 13
spaceplanes, 25
steam locomotive, 28, 30
storm watching, 17
Sunway TaihuLight computer,
 11

thermal imaging cameras, 17
Tsunami warning, 20

virtual reality, 26
volcano warning, 21

The Author

John Farnon is Royal Literary Fellow at City&Guilds in London, UK, and the author of a huge number of books for adults and children on science, technology, and history, including such international best-sellers as *Do Not Open* and *Do You Think You're Clever?* He has been shortlisted six times for the Royal Society's Young People's Book Prize, for titles such as *How the Earth Works* and *What Happens When?*

The Illustrator

Self-taught comic artist Joe Matthews drew Ivy The Terrible, Ball Boy, and Billy Whizz stories for the *Beano* before moving on to *Tom and Jerry* and *Baby Looney Tunes* comics. He also worked as a storyboard artist on the BBC TV series, *Bob the Builder*. Joe has produced his own *Funny Monsters Comic* and in 2016, published his comic-strip version of the Charles Dickens favorite, *A Christmas Carol*. Joe lives in North Wales, UK, with his wife.

Picture credits

t = top, m = middle, b = bottom, l = left, r = right

Shutterstock: 927 Creation 27tr; Anton Gvozdikov 16mr; catwalker 29br; Chaplin 9tl; Chesky 7tr; chombosan 7ml; Dmitry Chulov 13br; Donatas Dabravolskas 6ml; Everett Historical 29tl; Heiti Paves 13ml; Igor Barin 17ml; IgorGolovniov 28mr; jennyt 29tr; ksenia_bravo 27ml; Lisa S. 21br; Lukasz Pawel Szczepanski 24br; MriMan 22br; nadi555 29mr; Ociacia 7br; Romolo Tavani 19bl; Scharfsinn 6br; A.Sontaya 29bl; tichr 28br; Vandrage Artist 26b; Wlad74 28tl; woverwolf 28bl.

Wikimedia Commons: 9br, 30br.

Every effort has been made to trace the copyright holders. And we acknowledge in advance for any unintentional omissions. We would be pleased to insert the appropriate acknowledgment in any subsequent edition of this publication.